T0353755

Copyright © 2016 Eric K. Sorensen.

All rights reserved. No part of this book may be used or reproduced by any means, graphic, electronic, or mechanical, including photocopying, recording, taping or by any information storage retrieval system without the written permission of the author except in the case of brief quotations embodied in critical articles and reviews.

iUniverse books may be ordered through booksellers or by contacting:

iUniverse
1663 Liberty Drive
Bloomington, IN 47403
www.iuniverse.com
1-800-Authors (1-800-288-4677)

Because of the dynamic nature of the Internet, any web addresses or links contained in this book may have changed since publication and may no longer be valid. The views expressed in this work are solely those of the author and do not necessarily reflect the views of the publisher, and the publisher hereby disclaims any responsibility for them.

Any people depicted in stock imagery provided by Thinkstock are models, and such images are being used for illustrative purposes only. Certain stock imagery © Thinkstock.

ISBN: 978-1-5320-0807-8 (sc)
ISBN: 978-1-5320-0808-5 (e)

Library of Congress Control Number: 2016916159

Print information available on the last page.

iUniverse rev. date: 10/25/2016

The Witsdom of Mustafa Ali

Edited by

Eric K. Sorensen

iUniverse Publications

Marengo, WI

2016

Table of Contents

I. Poetry

II. Stories

III. Witsdom

(All photos used by permission)

Acknowledgements

Words fail when I attempt to express my gratitude to all those, so very many, who have guided and supported me along my journey.. My parents and grandparents, teachers from my youth, gurus of many statures (many of whom had no idea of the gifts they provided me). I must name my dear friend Hosain Mosevat, a brilliant Sufi poet who has inspired much of the poetry you will find within these pages.

I must also single out Kenton & Rebecca - if you know them, you do not need their last names, and if you do not, it does not matter. It was they who encouraged me to come out into the world, wherefore I had been perfectly content to sit at home with my music and books. The utter joy I have experienced by sharing Sufi tales and poetry with hundreds and hundreds of friends, new & old, over the past ten and more years would not have been possible without them.

And that brings me to this acknowledgement: to the many wonderful visitors to my tent. You have shared your precious time with me, laughed in all the right places of my stories, listened intently as I have read poetry or recited tales or performed on one of my musical instruments. Because you have allowed me into your hearts, I humbly ask once more for your attention with this volume of verse, tales, and some bits of what I choose to call "witsdom."

Much Love Always, Mustafa Ali

Introduction

I first became acquainted with Mustafa Ali in my days at Ripon College, where we shared a class in Eastern Literature (taught by Dr. Daniel Delekas, PhD), and an interest in Sufi thought. We stayed in touch through the decades since, and he was a particularly useful resource for my book, *New Tales of Nasrudin* (iUniverse 2006). When he was invited to begin making public appearances, he asked for my assistance as his "roadie," and it has been my great privilege to have been his close companion these past years. He continues to inspire me with his humor and wisdom.

This book is not meant to be read cover-to-cover, but rather to be picked up and thumbed through randomly, a few pages at a time. As Mustafa tells us:

Wisdom is like soda pop: if you consume too much at one time, you are likely to emit a loud belching noise!

The layout, font, and text color are designed for a calm, pleasant reading experience. Take your time; savor each thought and phrase, turn them over in your mind awhile. Enjoy.

To learn more about Sufi thought, I encourage the reader to find anything written by the late Dr. Idries Shah, the foremost interpreter of Sufism to the West.

May your never ending prayer be full of joy and dance!

Mustafa Ali is coming to town

I. Poetry

If Krishna had a car,

it would greet him

every morning,

covered in catalpa blossoms,

to be strewn

in his path

as he

travels

very far.

If Jesus had a jet,

it would be fueled

by Love,

contrails weaving

hope and spirit

to rain down

on

your head.

If Buddha had a boat,

it would sail

the eternal seas

of soul evolution,

plenty of room

for castaways

and those

who cannot float.

Lucifer has a locomotive,

stuck on the track

of ego,

greed,

and fear,

his passengers

looking out the windows

in vain,

still lighting

their votives.

I'm on the third stage

of my personal triathlon,

in no hurry

to reach the finish line,

nor am I sticking out

my thumb

to hitch a ride,

even at my age.

The Forces In the Universe

Science

tells us

there are 4 fundamental forces in the Universe:

Electromagnetism,

photons of every wavelength, the driving energy of all life;

The Strong Force and Weak Force,

which keep our atoms together and our planet from turning solid;

and Gravity,

keeping our world together

amidst

the Harmony of the Spheres.

Now,

they tell us,

there is Something New:

Dark Energy,

too mysterious to be part of the club,

and working in opposition to the other four,

and winning.

But there are 2 Forces

that Science cannot yet measure:

The first is Karma, which works throughout the Universe

(if you can understand the Karma of subatomic particles,
you are paying very close attention indeed!),

and the last,

and most powerful,

is Love.

How else to explain this thin biofilm on the skin of a rocky planet
with a magnetic field, orbited by a large satellite, lying within
the water zone of a solar system that is not bombarded with
gamma rays, occupying less than .1% of the planet's volume...?

How else?

Science tells us

it is all random happenstance,

that Love is a pheromonal delusion or wistful fantasy.

If so,

I choose the madness of Hafiz,

and embrace Love.

But perhaps

the belief in Randomness

is madness.

A good place to start

to sort all this out

would be

a scientific study

on

the Karma of Gravity.

An ancient outcrop

of granite,

covered with microbes,

some of which

cooperate

to form

lichen,

extracting minerals from the rock,

forming

just enough

soil

for moss to take hold.

A fern

waves

overhead,

shading a fungus,

and

a blade of grass,

and a bit of

clover.

Nearby

a berry bush

sits

on the edge

of a forest.

This is not

unlike

the Evolution

of

an Idea.

Old Souls

Do you know who you are?

I don't mean your name...

It was many times before

and I'm sure you're the same

One who touched my life;

It's good to see you, my friend.

Old Soul, our time is here again.

From the first time we met

(I can't explain how I knew),

But even from the back

I could tell that it was You,

and now we've got another chance;

Let's make the most of it today:

Old Soul, we're bound to find our way.

I want you to know

that I mean you No Harm;

But should you choose to go

Consider this: The next time you are charmed

by someone's eyes, you've met a friend from lives past.

Old Soul, the truth will come at last.

We are all old souls,

Wandering through our lives.

Sometimes we have been husbands,

Sometimes we have been wives,

and sometimes we've believed

we were completely on our own.

Old Soul, you will never be alone.

Do you know who you are?

I don't mean your name.

It's been so many times before,

and I'm sure you are the same

Ones who touched my lives,

It's so good to see you, my friends!

Old Souls, our time is here again.

Old Souls, our time will come again.

It takes

All

the Seven Seas

to float

my canoe.

Air

is piled up

seven miles deep

around the globe

so I can breathe.

A planet's worth

of gravity

keeps me

from leaving

this world.

Where I come from,

Hafiz teaches

mountain climbing;

Mullah Nasrudin

gives me

a wink,

or a scowl,

every now & then.

I measure

my time

against

the Entirety

of the Universe;

and realize

that I am

insignificantly

unique.

That much love

is

More than I expected.

Time

is different

for

the animals:

They understand

the rhythm

of seasons,

tides,

day & night,

the ebb & flow

of predator

and prey.

Time

is stranger

for

the mountains:

uplift,

erosion,

earthquakes

and glaciers

punctuate

their day.

The world

knows little,

and cares less,

about

vacations,

bus schedules,

and

the price

of stock.

There is no god,

no flag,

no uniform nor badge,

no code of honor,

no state,

no revenge,

no power

that can assume

responsibility

for

an act of

violence.

There is only

the one

who performs

the act,

the responsibility

being

his or hers

alone.

I have a great friend named Hosain

Who sports a beautiful silky white mane,

He reads Sufi verse

And the whole Universe

Stands on its head, going happily insane!!

If you've never had a friend

for whom

you would

drive a thousand miles

for a birthday

or a command performance;

with whom

you freely travel

the two-way street

of loving criticism;

with whom

you stay up until all hours,

trading poems, songs,

and dirty jokes;

with whom

no silence is uncomfortable;

to whom

you open your heart,

only to find

an open heart

waiting;

if you've never had a friend

like that,

get one!

I had a Dream

that I went 2000 years

into the Future.

The People then

will have a

Religion

in which

Dr. Martin Luther King

will be

the central figure.

The entire society

will practice

Non-Violent Conflict Resolution.

Many of the devout

adorn themselves

with tiny gold earrings

and pendants

in the shape of the Noose.

I find myself

unable

to correct

their anachronism.

A raindrop formed in a cloud,

a bit of water held together with dust.

Gravity beckoned,

and the drop

(named Pirr)

began its journey to Earth.

Of course,

in the mind of Pirr,

Earth was more like Heaven:

the inevitable, universal fate of most raindrops;

something mysterious and unknowable,

for no drop had ever returned

with a description.

Pirr continued to descend,

blown this way and that.

Pirr imagined

that these deviations from the strictly vertical course

were matters of free will;

but how much insight,

not to mention outsight,

can you expect?

We are, after all,

speaking of nothing more than a raindrop,

are we not?

Finally,

SPLAT!!!

Pirr reached Earth/Heaven

and was annihilated,

but

the water

joined

the water

from other former raindrops

to gather into a rivulet, a stream, a river, an ocean,

traveling in and out of trillions of life forms

in water,

on land,

even in the clouds.

And eventually,

sooner for some than for others,

water is lifted into the sky as vapor

to gather into clouds

to make more rain.

I know this because

it was told to me

by a solar particle

that had been passing by

and got caught in Earth's magnetic field,

and saw

the whole

thing.

It is not an easy thing

to tolerate

a bigot.

Try

saying to them,

even if only in your Heart:

"Because

I love you,

I wish for you

the Joy,

the healthy exercise

of your

Soul,

that you can

Experience

when

you truly

get to know

someone

very different

from yourself."

Mindfulness

I am

aware

of myself.

I am aware

of my awareness

of myself.

And now I am aware

of my awareness

of my awareness of myself.

Am I going deeper,

or

just

adding

layers?

<u>Travel Haiku</u>

Pieces of soul

Left ev'rywhere I go.

Good thing it's overflowing!

Water

A man suffered a mild stroke,

and recovered;

he experienced the odd side-effect

of forgetting

about water.

Caught in a sudden downpour,

he found his clothing transformed

from warm comfort

to clinging chill.

"Something so powerful and evil must be avoided,"

he told himself.

As his thirst grew,

he reasoned.

"This insidious liquid

forces me to a

Primal Need.

I must learn to coexist with it,

or perish without it."

As he drank,

in his haste

he splashed some drops

into his eyes and

up his nose.

The curse

that passed his lips

was no darker

than the one he carried within.

He became filthy,

certain that he would

slip in the bath;

and he was suspicious

that his laundered clothes

contained a trace

of water's

malice.

He kept a personal account

of drownings,

seeing that as

the worst of all possible deaths.

He could not abide

to eat fish,

creatures who spent their lifetime

immersed.

Friends and family

tried to "help" him

to see

the error of his ways.

But their efforts

succeeded only

in adding to his alienation.

Eventually

the cognitive dissonance

became too much,

and he died.

Thank goodness

this is only a story,

and that no such person

really exists.

Unless
you are at the very bottom
of the food chain, you exist
at the expense
of other life forms.
This
is the true meaning
of
Original Sin, and
the only
Grace
available to us
is
to
Love,
Love,
Love!

There's a hole in the bottom of my shoe,

There's a hole in the bottom of my shoe,

There's a hole, in the sole,

There's a hole in the bottom of my shoe.

I got water in the hole in the bottom of my shoe,

I got water in the hole in the bottom of my shoe,

I got water, I shouldn'ta ought'er,

I got water in the hole in the bottom of my shoe.

I got a chill from the water in the hole in the bottom of my shoe,

I got a chill from the water in the hole in the bottom of my shoe,

I got a chill, it was no thrill!

I got a chill from the water in the hole in the bottom of my shoe.

I got a fever from the chill from the water in
the hole in the bottom of my shoe,

I got a fever from the chill from the water in
the hole in the bottom of my shoe,

I got a fever, you better believe 'er,

I got a fever from the chill from the water in
the hole in the bottom of my shoe.

I took a pill for the fever from the chill from the
water in the hole in the bottom of my shoe,

I took a pill for the fever from the chill from the
water in the hole in the bottom of my shoe,

I took a pill, it made me ill!

I took a pill for the fever from the chill from the
water in the hole in the bottom of my shoe.

I got a bill for being ill from the pill for the fever from the
chill from the water in the hole in the bottom of my shoe,

I got a bill for being ill from the pill for the fever from the
chill from the water in the hole in the bottom of my shoe,

I got a bill, I'm payin' it still!

I got a bill for being ill from the pill for the fever from the
chill from the water in the hole in the bottom of my shoe.

So I sued for the bill from being ill from the pill for the fever from
the chill from the water in the hole in the bottom of my shoe,

So I sued for the bill from being ill from the pill for the fever from
the chill from the water in the hole in the bottom of my shoe,

So I sued, so would you!

So I sued for the bill from being ill from the pill for the fever from
the chill from the water in the hole in the bottom of my shoe.

I got another bill when I sued for the bill from being ill from the pill for the fever from the chill from the water in the hole in the bottom of my shoe,

I got another bill when I sued for the bill from being ill from the pill for the fever from the chill from the water in the hole in the bottom of my shoe,

I got another bill, I've had my fill!

I got another bill when I sued for the bill from being ill from the pill for the fever from the chill from the water in the hole in the bottom of my shoe,

So I fixed my shoe!

The same ancient genes

which

make us

fear

and strive

with each other

are related to

the genes

which

make us

listen

to nature

more closely.

Civilization fails

when

too many

of its citizens

go insane,

deprived
of the stimulus
necessary
to survive.

Some say,

"The Universe

is not

a friendly,

kind,

or welcoming

place";

which is all the more reason

to be

friendly,

kind,

and welcoming.

The Ballad of a Line

Consider the line

  As it passes through time:

It can't curve, it can't bend,

  No beginning or end.

Circles ask: "Line, how come you're so straight?"

  The line answers not, but his mind contemplates:

I once loved a curve,

  And to see her form swerve

Was to watch all mathematics in rhythm and rhyme.

But to her I was skew,

  And both of us knew

I could never be hers, and she never mine.

Oh, there have been others: Parabolas fair,

  Ellipses and circles; why, even a square!

At each union a point, poor orphan of math.

  It's its fate to suffer the formulae's wrath.

Dimension, direction, width, even weight,

  Are not its. It can't curve, it can't even go straight!

But those unions meant nothing; at least, not to me.

(That affair with $x^2 - y + 3z$!)

All those numbers and answers don't mean anything.

Just my Love, my Fair Curve, to Thee do I sing.

I've a dream,

But it seems

That I'll have to wait.

She a sine,

And all mine,

For I go on straight;

We dance for all Time, I with my mate,

As I pass through her curve to the end: Lazy 8.

The line goes his way, for it's naught but a dream.

Quite sad I must say, and unfair some will deem,

But it's Math, it won't change;

It's all prearranged.

Be you circle, ellipse, or just 2 + 2,

If the numbers aren't right, you're bound to get skewed!

It's easy

to do nice things for people

you care about.

After all,

what good is it

having people you care about

if you don't do

nice things for them?

To do nice things

for people you don't care about,

even

people you despise:

Now that's something!

But,

what's the good

of having people you despise,

if you're still going to do nice things for them?

Just

read that question again

for the answer.

If

You give me

Money,

I shall

Only

Spend it.

But,

When you give me

Your Time

and

Attention,

The most precious

Things

You Have to offer,

That is

Something

I will

Carry

In my Heart

Forever.

Have you ever noticed

how some people

have highly organized

outer lives, while their inner lives

are in turmoil?

Or,

perhaps you know someone

who has attained inner peace,

but whose outer life

is chaotic?

Of course,

we all know those

whose entire world is a complete mess,

and we have at least heard of

those few

who have attained

inner and outer

Perfection.

We engage

in a constant,

seemingly hopeless struggle

against gravity & entropy,

trying to control

the elements

within & without

us.

But

Love

is

different.

Love is chaotic,

and

has its own sort

of flowing order.

Love

embraces

the messiness of our souls,

and

the dangerous world around us.

Love

reminds us

that Life

is a statistically insignificant

aberration

in

the

Universe.

Human Nature

is

to be

Joyful,

to appreciate

Beauty,

and

to help

Others

in Need...

and,

sometimes,

to try

to find

a Good Excuse

for Bad

Behavior.

When I think

of

my troubles,

my struggles,

my mistakes

and

misperceptions;

despite

my many blessings,

my health,

my strength,

my intelligence,

my Spirit,

my friends...

I begin to understand

how

the cumulative effect

of

7 billion

struggles,

mistakes,

and

misperceptions

ends up

on

the evening news.

Who Am I?

Am I What Others See?

If So, How well do I see

What

Others See?

Am I What I See?

If So,

What do I do

About

What I See?

Am I What I Do?

If So,

What do I say

About

What I Do?

Am I What I Say?

If So,

What do I believe

About

What I Say?

Am I What I Believe?

If So,

What do I love

About

What I Believe?

Am I What I Love?

If So,

What do I think

About

What I Love?

Am I What I Think?
If So,
What do I learn
About
What I Think?

Am I What I Learn?
If So,
How does it help me Know
Who
I
Am?

There is an infinite

number of

dimensionless points

between any two locations,

even

crowded into

a Planck.

In the math

of the Mind,

There is

always

an infinity

between us.

But

in the calculation

of the Heart,

we

are

never

apart.

Mustafa Ali is not in his tent

II. Stories

Death Says 'Happy Birthday'

A young man, a fine, kind, intelligent young man, the kind of man who you know will achieve great things in life, was stricken with a severe illness on the day of his birthday upon which he entered adulthood. As he laid in his bed, feverish and delirious, he was visited by Death.

"I can end all this pain for you. You need only come with me."

"I'm not ready to die," said the young man. "I have so much to look forward to, so much promise in my life."

"Very well," said Death. "I'll just take someone else. It is a small matter."

The young man shortly recovered from his illness, and dismissed the visitation as a fragment of a fevered mind, even when he learned that one of the oldest members of his village had passed away around the time he had been ill.

He had nearly put the entire incident out of his mind by his next birthday. He was away at school, his friends had thrown him a big party, and he had attained a fairly deep state of intoxication by the time he collapsed into bed. And suddenly there was Death again, sitting on the edge of his bed.

"Are you ready to come with me?" was all he said.

"What? No, no, go away! I'm not coming with you. I'm having too much fun!"

"That's alright, I'll just take someone else," and Death was gone.

The next day the young man tried to tell some of his friends about his hallucination, but when they all retreated with strange looks and muttering,

"Why would you want to talk about that? That's so morbid!"; he learned to keep the topic to himself.

On his next birthday he purposely stayed on a narrow, sober path, much to the amusement of his friends, who each tried to declare possession of his "share" of the drinks and smokes. And, for good measure, he had a young lady accompany him to bed so he would not be alone. After a most satisfying romp, and just as he was about to fall asleep, there was Death again. His partner had fallen asleep.

"Are you ready to come with me now?"

"Are you kidding? I'm just getting into the prime of my life! No! Why do you keep coming back?"

"That's alright, I'll just take someone else," was all Death said.

The young man knew better than to talk to anyone this time, even after some pointed inquiries.

The next year the young man found himself in the military, and in a combat zone on his birthday. As he hunkered down, with bullets zipping inches above his head, he nevertheless felt a strange calmness, and Death was there.

"How about now?" said Death.

"My squad needs me. My country needs me. I don't want to die!"

"That's alright, I'll just take someone else," and Death was gone, but not far.

*****

The young man developed a brilliant combat and military career, performing numerous acts of courage under fire, fearless and seemingly invincible. Only his closest friends noticed a slight downturn in his demeanor each year as his birthday approached, and he developed a strange habit of looking up casualty lists and obituaries for a week or two afterwards. He lived life with a zeal and a zest that others found inspiring and enviable. When he retired from his military career he was immediately accepted into the world of business, where he amassed a fortune and rose to become a pillar in his community. And no matter what, every year he was visited by Death, who offered him the same choice, which he refused, and to which Death responded with the same phrase. It had become an almost meaningless ritual, like blowing out the candles on his cake; and yet, he somehow looked forward to the annual opportunity to defy Death, and the fact that someone else was destined to take his place became something that, as he told himself, *I can live with.*

By the time he was a robustly healthy nearly seventy year-old, he was regarded by all, including himself, as a man with an abundance of blessings: material, familial, and even spiritual. His many children and grandchildren were already making their marks in life. One of his daughters was head of a foundation that provided many charitable services in the community. Another was a doctor, and his first son had followed his military path, and *his* son had just enlisted.

As he waited in his den office for his birthday *pas de deux*, he began to think about how he was going to change the routine. And there was Death.

"Are you ready? Your aging body will face steadily increasing infirmities, you will see an accelerating number of losses of your friends and cohorts, and a noticeable decline in your mental faculties. You won't have to go through any of that if you come with me now."

"Before I answer," said the man. "I have a question: Who would take my place? Is that something I'm allowed to know?"

"I can tell you," said Death, "but you're not going to like it."

In an instant he knew the answer before Death said a word, as I'm sure you have also figured. This is not a complicated story. In that instant, fifty years of uncertainty, fear, survivor's guilt, pride, and entitlement all came to the surface like a stew boiling over the kettle.

"Why him?!" he cried. "Why my grandson?"

He became angry. "This is the cruelty of Death! Is this how you punish me for playing this game you put before me so many years ago? You made it so easy: All I had to do was say 'No' and I got to live another year. What about the ones who replaced me? Did they get a choice? Why me? Why him?"

"That is much more than one question. Time is short. I must have your answer."

And that is where this story ends.

If you think you know how the man answers, you might want to wait until Death knocks on *your* door.

Tea For Two

The young warrior approached the small hut in which his enemy resided. His years of training, experience in warfare, and many months of tracking down the whereabouts of his foe had all led to this final set of moments. He had spent hours hidden and watching the house, and had learned the old priest's routine: as dusk gathered, the old man would light a lantern and a fire to boil some tea.

Tonight was no different, and as the faint glow from inside became apparent, and the smell of the wood smoke touched his nostrils, he made his move. He would have the advantage, coming from the dark into the light, and he meant to strike quickly, as soon as the old man opened his door.

As he approached the front of the house, however, he realized that dark or no, not many people would open their door to someone wielding a sword, so he slipped it back in its sheath. *I can strike soon enough once I am inside*, he told himself.

Just as he was about to knock, the door flew open. The younger man jumped back, expecting an attack, but instead the old man laughed gently and said, "There you are! I've been expecting you. Please, please, come in!"

The confused warrior entered, and the priest said, "Welcome to my humble dwelling. Is it customary in your land for guests to carry their swords inside their host's home, or do you lay your weapons outside the door, as we do here?"

The young man mumbled something and, to his own amazement, laid his sword against the wall outside the doorway. His smiling host then led him to a cushion and invited him to sit. "It will be a few moments before the tea is ready," and sat himself at arm's length directly in front of his guest.

"You have come a long way, my young friend, and now that you have found me, do you still intend to kill me?"

"I must," answered the warrior, feeling as if he were stuck in a dream. There was an odd tingling sensation at the top of his forehead.

"Oh, yes, yes, of course!" The old priest chuckled. "Such certainty of purpose! I'm sure it has served you well many times, and as a result you have developed the delusion that your certitude gives you a deeper understanding of what is true."

The warrior felt a quick flush of anger and reached for the sword at his side before realizing that it was not there. Just then the tea began to boil.

"Do you like your tea sweetened?"

The young man seemed to emerge from his trance. "Why are we speaking of tea?" he said, his voice shaking in a way that did not seem familiar. "I am here to end your life!"

"Unless you must be somewhere right away, I think there is time to share some tea."

"But are you not afraid?"

"Afraid? Why?"

"Because I am here to kill you!"

"Yes, you said that already. There is no need to raise your voice."

"But do you not fear death?"

"Do *you* fear death? You have certainly done enough of Death's work in your life."

"I am a warrior. I am prepared to die at every moment! Do not speak to *me* of fear!"

"If you have no fear, why do you need to prepare?" said the old man with a shrug.

The warrior's mouth opened, but nothing came out. His host rocked back and forth with gentle laughter. "I will sweeten your tea a little extra," he said, and got up to prepare the beverage.

The young man had become preoccupied with the priest's question, and was nearly finished with his tea before he realized that nothing had been said for several minutes. He found his host looking intently into his eyes.

"So you still intend to kill me?"

"I do."

"Well, for now we are just sitting, sipping tea, and sharing a conversation. I would be very interested to understand your reasons for this mission."

"You are dangerous. Your ideas will infect others, which will lead to disorder and suffering."

"Which ideas, in particular?"

"Your cowardly disavowal of violence in all forms. If conflicts are not settled with strength, by definition the weak will have power; and weak men cannot govern: they are meant to be ruled by the strong. Violence is part of human nature, and to deny it is a form of perversion."

"Such absolute judgment! You seem to have given this a great deal of thought. I am curious: Did these ideas form while you were engaged in violence, or was it during the quiet times in between?"

"The truth was obvious to me as I carried out my beliefs in action..."

"So the belief was there before the action?"

"I-I suppose so..."

"And it was in those moments of peaceful contemplation that you arrived at your 'truth' of human nature."

The tingling returned to top of the warrior's forehead. He reached up to scratch.

"What will happen, my thoughtful young friend, when you realize that all violence is merely the result of a lack of imagination?"

There was now a slight ringing in the young man's ears. His head began to swim. *Could I have been poisoned? Could this priest be capable of such treachery and still espouse his beliefs?* In the next moment his head cleared, and again he found his host staring directly at him, a look of concern on his face.

"Are you all right, my friend? Have I put too much sweetening in the tea?"

At this the warrior lunged toward his target, reaching for the old man's throat. His fingers closed on air as the priest swiftly ducked back and in a smooth, twisting motion got to his feet as the warrior sprawled onto the floor.

"Goodness! I hope you are not hurt!"

"Does humiliation count?"

Suddenly they were both laughing out loud, full belly laughs, with tears rolling down their cheeks. It became a mutual fit of laughter, until both were gasping for breath.

"So...*huff*...do you still intend to...*huff*...kill me?"

"*Hooo...Absolutely...heee...*"

Contented sigh. "I admire the strength of your convictions, even though I cannot accept their validity. I must say that if today is to be my last day, I am glad it is spent with you."

"Why would you say such a thing?"

"Well, clearly you are a warrior of honor and great skill, you do not seem cruel, and you are acting on your beliefs. Also, you have been a delightful guest. Death can be a very intimate experience, as you well know."

The ringing was back. The warrior finally recognized his sensations as the anticipation he had had before his very first battlefield, at the age of nearly fourteen. Another soldier five years his senior had told him, *Today is a good day to die. But even better to live!!* Later that day the boy, now battle-tested and only slightly bloodied, had seen his comforter hacked to pieces by a group of enemies. He and his comrades were able to prevail, exacting their revenge on their rivals.

"I must get my sword," he blurted out. "Will you come outside to face me, or will you cower in your hut?" His bravado felt hollow, as if he were acting a role.

"Well, I do not wish to leave a mess here for others to clean, so if you will permit me to tidy up our tea, I will join you shortly."

As the warrior waited outside in the gathering dark, doubt began to creep into his resolve. *This man has shown me nothing but kindness. In my heart I accused him of treachery, when it was my own fear that had got hold of me. Is my belief in the need for violence blinding me to choices that could be equally viable?*

His thoughts were interrupted as the door of the hut opened and a figure emerged wearing an outlandish assortment of antique and homemade armor, mostly made of wood, leather, and padding. He wore a helmet that was flat and conical, and he carried what looked like a five foot staff of some sort of flexible wood.

Training and instinct took over, and the young man rushed his opponent, ready to deliver a killing blow. Again, he found only air, lost his balance, and tumbled forward. This time he rolled back up into a defensive position, only to see the old man gently laughing and leaning on his staff, fifteen feet away. The warrior approached more slowly this time, and adopted a more classic stance. But each time he attacked he missed every blow, or it was slapped aside by the wooden staff. This went on for some time, and the sound of the *whoosh* of his blade and the occasional *clack* of wood on steel was punctuated by the warrior's increasingly labored breathing and the old priest's gentle laughter.

After he had fallen to the ground for what seemed like the twentieth time, he threw down his sword. "Why won't you stand still and fight?!?"

"Well, I am not afraid of death, but I do enjoy life! Did you expect me to lay my head on a chopping block for you?"

"But your speed and agility have presented you with many opportunities to give me a good whack with your stick. Why haven't you?"

"You must know that I truly mean you no harm."

"How did you learn such an art?"

"I am sure you know that I could never teach it to a man of violence."

At these words, tears flooded the eyes of the warrior and he fell to his knees. "Master! Please, teach me!"

And so the young man became the pupil, and he learned well. The woods around their little hut often rang with laughter well into the night. When the old man finally left this world, the younger took his place. And one day, late in his life, he became aware that a young warrior was seeking him out, to dispatch him in the name of the Efficacy of Violence.

COMPASSION

Nasrudin was walking his bicycle down a path in the park when a young man approached him and said, "Can I borrow your bicycle?"

"No, I don't think so," said the Mullah.

"Oh, so you think I'm going to steal it?" said the youth.

"Certainly not!" said Nasrudin. "It's just that I couldn't put upon you the burden of protecting my bicycle on my behalf! After all, there may be thieves about; you said so yourself!"

MANY LIVES

A Buddhist friend of Nasrudin commented on the numerous roles and jobs Nasrudin had had in his life: teacher, baker, counselor to royalty, donkey trader, etc.

"Yes, well," said the Mullah, "Just in case this reincarnation thing doesn't work out, I'm going to try to live all my lives this time around."

DAYLIGHT SAVINGS TIME

Nasrudin was pleased when he heard that the government had issued an edict to move the clocks forward one hour in the late winter, as an energy-saving measure.

"Brilliant!!" he exclaimed. "The extra hour of sunlight in the afternoon will help the snow melt faster!"

AMAZING!

"I am constantly amazed," said the Mullah, "at my ability to be constantly amazed!"

HAPPY BIRTHDAY

"Mullah, there has been a study which indicates that more and more people under the age of 60 are having strokes."

"How fortunate for me!" declared Nasrudin. "I just turned 61!"

Mustafa Ali and his Tibetan singing bowl

III. Witsdom

The Witsdom of Mustafa Ali

When you cannot laugh at yourself, you are in serious trouble!

I am glad we scheduled the meeting for next Tuesday instead of yesterday, or we would have missed it.

As I get older, I realize that this is an awfully long time to be myself, and not nearly enough time with the people about whom I care.

Hatred is a luxury I cannot afford.

Where am I from? This morning I woke up in my bed.

A young lady once said to me, "Mustafa, I love your voice!"

I replied, "Well, I am sorry, but you cannot have it! I need it to communicate; and besides, it would seem silly coming out of your mouth!"

Many people work hard so that their children need not, but what are we supposed to do with all those lazy children?

I am self-employed; which means my boss is a jerk and I cannot get good help!

I experienced a lot of things when I was younger...this morning.

Ah, my dear friend! It is so good to finally meet you!!

I am completely unqualified to judge the moral
character of anyone, especially myself!

Each day is a gift: Have fun unwrapping it!

Looking forward to your last breath is much easier than looking back on it!

I enjoy supporting losing sports teams: they bring so
much happiness to so many different cities!

I am very independent-minded: I don't even heed my own advice.

I have never been poor, but I have been chronically short of funds for most of my life.

Christianity and Communism are actually pretty good ideas... It's too bad hardly anyone one has ever actually tried them!

If teenagers were not obnoxious, the human race would have died out long ago.

As a devout agnostic, I do not understand the need for people to believe in fairy tales in order to behave themselves.

We can fly only when we are not stuck on the ground chasing the bottom line.

The troubles of humanity make more sense when you realize that, by definition, the majority of people are average or below.

When you say to someone, "My Imaginary Friend can beat up your Imaginary Friend," it makes your Imaginary Friend very sad.

Freedom is the ability to determine for oneself what takes place on the inside and the outside of one's head.

Before one condemns *Popeye The Sailor Man*® as an example of a vegetarian diet leading to violence, it is important to remember that he is just a cartoon.

I am making the best use of the holes in my head in order
to avoid having someone decide I need another one.

Life is an uphill struggle, especially when you are going downhill.

It has been lovely having you all visit. Now please get out.

Logically speaking, using logic to disprove an illogical opinion is illogical.

I have the strength of ten men. Unfortunately, they are all in their 90's, and some of them are asking for it back.

An open mind is a rare welcome.

Imagine tolerance and cooperation; see what happens.

The mosquito egg can lie dormant for seven years before hatching to annoy the world.

Peaceful revolution is both the means and the end.

It is difficult not to be an impatient patient,
but not as difficult as being one...

I "identify" as a human being. Any other label is for your benefit, not mine.

Humans are wonderful at multi-tasking: We provide, food,
shelter, and transport to billions of microbes!

I have studied Zen juggling for many years: I
am now up to *eleven* imaginary balls!

If your values can't withstand scrutiny from others,
it is time for scrutiny from within.

Campaigning politicians have the difficult task of demonstrating
to the voters that they are the most convincing liar.

When a photon enters your pupil, having travelled from
the heart of a star, its journey is just beginning.

I'm beginning to realize that I'm not as good as
I used to be...in fact, I never was!

Love will get you through times of no money better than
money will get you through times of no love.

Injustice can lead to revolution. We need less of it...
or more, depending on your point of view.

Everything is difficult until you know how to do it.

That a species with a superstitious framework for understanding
the world, armed to the teeth with nuclear weapons, has survived
this long is an indication that we are evolving just enough and
in the nick of time to avoid extinction...or, it's a miracle!

Anger is a dangerous weapon, causing more harm
to the wielder than to the target.

There are people who have been dead for years, but just
don't have the good manners to lie down and be quiet.

My business card advises the holder to contact me "by Telepathy." Since
I began handing them out, my mind has been ringing off the hook!

In all my travels, the most wondrous sight I've ever beheld was this morning's light.

Everything is a prayer. You can have angry prayers, violent prayers, healing prayers, loving prayers, learning prayers. It's up to you.

You have already made a difference in the world by being born, but you needn't stop there.

Technology has taught us that our planet is much smaller, and there's more room for all of us, than we used to imagine.

Every once in a while we ignore the insistent distractions of our bellies, balls, and egos, and actually pay close attention to what is happening around us.

If human stupidity is not a survival skill, why is there so much of it?

A smile can bounce around inside your head for years!

We spend far more time worrying about what others think of us than others spend thinking of us.

One of the first sentences spoken in human speech was, "Wait until you have children of your own."

An ant can describe an elephant better than a human can define God.

Productivity is overrated.

Wisdom is like soda pop: if you take in too much at once,
you are likely to emit a loud belching noise.

Between gravity and entropy, we haven't got a chance.

The harp string cannot make its beautiful music without tension.

I used to get depressed over how unhappy I was,
until I learned to celebrate my joy.

Love for others is the crucial difference between
an Enlightened One and a psychopath.

You cannot cure shame by trying to share it.

I do not entirely trust my mouth: it will do
nearly anything to get what it wants.

Knowing when to let go is a skill worth hanging onto.

Doing well and doing good need not be mutually exclusive activities.

If we can only develop wealth by poisoning our planet, perhaps we are not as intelligent as we like to think we are.

Waiting until your chickens come home to roost is not
a good time to decide you do not like chicken.

Anger does not make ignorance smarter.

Our enemies have an ingenious plan: they are going to let us
continue to keep doing what we have been doing to ourselves.

I am a very tolerant person: I have put up with myself all this time!

When I was a young man I would feel great pain in my heart whenever I heard of others' misfortunes. Then I noticed that my sorrow was affecting those around me, so that my response to the suffering of others was creating even *more* suffering in the world! For some time after that, I responded in the opposite manner: first of all rejoicing that the suffering was not my own, and allowing myself some indulgences to celebrate my good fortune. Well! It was soon made clear to me that this was not appropriate. So now, whenever I hear of the suffering of others, I ask myself if I can do anything to help, and if so, I will with joy in my heart; but if not, then I go about my business as before.

Mustafa Ali & Yuri Chafkin

Printed in the United States
by Baker & Taylor Publisher Services